The Weather
WIND

Terry Jennings

Chrysalis Children's Books

First published in the UK in 2004 by
Chrysalis Children's Books
An imprint of Chrysalis Books Group PLC
The Chrysalis Building, Bramley Road, London W10 6SP

ISBN 1 84458 071 7

British Library Cataloguing in Publication Data
for this book is available from the British Library.

Produced by Bender Richardson White

Editorial Manager: Joyce Bentley
Project Editors: Lionel Bender and Clare Lewis
Designer: Ben White
Production: Kim Richardson
Picture Researcher: Cathy Stastny
Cover Make-up: Mike Pilley, Radius

Printed in China

10 9 8 7 6 5 4 3 2 1

Words in **bold** can be found in New words on page 31.

Picture credits and copyrights
Corbis Images Inc.: cover (Mark Gamba) and page 17 (Chinch Gryniewicz/Ecoscene). Ecoscene:
pages 8 (Chinch Gryniewicz), 10 (Martin Jones), 14 (Norman Rout), 15 (Nick Hawkes), 16
(Papilio/Robert Pickett), 18 (Vicki Coombs), 19 (Frank Blackburn), 20 (Anthony Cooper), 22 (Jim
Winkley), 23 (Genevieve Leaper), 25 (Chinch Gryniewicz), 27 (Stuart Baines). PhotoDisc Inc.: pages
2 (Emma Lee/Life File), 5 (David Toase), 26 (Adam Crowley), 28 (Jeremy Woodhouse), 29 (Jeremy
Woodhouse). Rex Features Ltd.: pages 6 (Ian Jones), 9 (Frank Siteman), 13 (Palmbeach Post). Steve
Gorton: pages 4, 7, 21. Terry Jennings: page 24. Weatherstock: pages 1, 11, 12.

Contents

What is wind?

Wind is moving **air**. You cannot see the wind, but you can feel it blowing against you.

You can hear the wind and see it blowing leaves and flags.

Against the wind

It is hard to walk in a strong wind. The wind pushes against you.

The wind also makes you feel cold, even on a sunny day.

Breezes

A gentle wind is called a **breeze**. A breeze makes tree leaves rustle.

You can feel a breeze blowing gently on your skin. It makes soap bubbles float away.

Gale force

There are strong winds in a **gale**. They can make large waves and push you over as you walk.

Gale winds can break the branches of trees and blow down old trees.

Hurricanes

The strongest wind is called a **hurricane**. It can blow down walls and turn over cars.

A very strong hurricane can even blow down houses.

Wind direction

A **weather vane** shows which way the wind is blowing.

So does a **windsock** at an airport. A wind blowing from the north is called a north wind.

Blowing seeds

A dandelion seed has a fluffy top. The fluffy top helps the seed to float on the wind.

Sycamore seeds have little wings. The wings turn in the wind.

Windfall

The wind blows ripe fruit hanging in trees to the ground. These are called **windfalls**.

Windfalls of nuts and berries from trees are picked up by birds and squirrels.

Drying wind

Winds pick up water as they blow. These clothes are drying in the wind.

After it rains, wind and sun together dry the fields.

Flying in the wind

You can fly a kite on a windy day. Some birds use the wind to lift them high in the sky.

A seagull can fly without
moving its wings when it
is lifted by the wind.

Moved by wind

Yachts and other boats with **sails** are pushed along by winds. Balloons are blown in the air by winds.

These sand yachts are pushed
along the beach by the wind.

Windmills

The wind can push round the arms of a **windmill**. Windmills are used to grind corn.

Now we use special windmills to make electricity. These are called wind **turbines**.

Wind action

These hills of sand are called **sand dunes**. They were shaped by the wind.

Some hard rocks, like these in the United States, have also been shaped by the wind.

Quiz

1 What is the wind made of?

2 What is a gentle wind called?

3 What is the strongest wind called?

4 Where does a north wind blow from?

5 How are dandelion seeds carried to new places?

6 Which kinds of boats are pushed along by the wind?

7 What do we use windmills for?

8 What type of windmills make electricity?

The answers are all in this book!

New words

air the invisible mixture of gases that surrounds us and which we breathe.

breeze a gentle wind.

gale a strong wind.

hurricane a very strong wind that causes great damage.

sail a sheet of material to catch the wind to help something move forward or round.

sand dune a large hill made of sand and shaped by the wind.

turbine an engine that spins round and is powered by flowing water, wind or steam.

weather vane a pointer on the top of a building showing which way the wind is blowing.

windfall fruit blown from a tree by the wind on to the ground.

windmill a building with a sail moved by the wind that turns a mill or powers a pump.

windsock a long tube that changes shape and direction as wind blows through it; it is used for showing which way the wind is blowing.

Index